Case Studies in Entrepreneurship - Vol. 1

Tejas Subrahmanya

Dedicated to my parents
Dr. M R Subrahmanya and Mrs. C K Mahalakshmi

Preface

This book is a compilation of business plans that was developed by my students at Delhi Business School, APG Shimla University and IIT Mandi.

I always had the idea of writing a book on entrepreneurship, but not the regular information that most books provide. Writing a case study book seemed very feasible, given that I have already taught entrepreneurship at Delhi Business School, APG Shimla University and IIT Mandi and this has led to the development of a number of business plans.

The book is designed from an academic perspective and the ideas are not meant to be copied by others, and all intellectual property of the respective teams has been acknowledged. However, as with all businesses, most ideas are an improvement of an existing concept, and readers are welcome to improve upon the ideas that are presented in the book. One advice I would like to give our readers is to ensure that the IP acknowledged here is not copied literally and necessary due diligence is made before using specific concepts, terms and other IP. This is necessary so as to avoid any IP infringement.

There are questions at the end of each case study. I would urge you to review the questions, so that you can get an idea of how these business ideas could be improved upon.

These business plans have not yet been implemented, i.e. they are not yet seen the light of the day, but a few of the students who developed the business plans have already got plans to ensure that they start their ventures in the next year or two.

Acknowledgement

I would like to acknowledge all my students who have put in a lot of effort in developing these business plans.

I would also like to acknowledge Prof. Bhavender Paul who helped me in organizing the course in Entrepreneurship at IIT Mandi. Without his help and encouragement, this book could not have been completed.

I would also like to thank the management of APG Shimla University, the Hon'ble Ex-Vice Chancellor Prof. (Dr.) Devendra Pathak and Ex-Head – School of Management, Prof. Ravi Prakash for giving me an opportunity to deliver the course on entrepreneurship to the MBA students who chose entrepreneurship as their stream specialization.

I would like to thank Prof. Rajeev Roy, Associate Professor at Xavier's Institute of Management, Bhubaneshwar for reviewing this book and providing his valuable comments.

Finally, I would like to thank the erstwhile management of Delhi Business School for helping me to teach the students of BBA entrepreneurship so that they could set up their campus company.

I would also like to thank my family members who have given me the strength to develop this into a book.

Table of Contents

Badarpur ke Mashoor Salad Wale

Badarpur ke Mashoor Salad Wale was set up as a campus company at Delhi Business School, New Delhi. The concept of a salad bar within a campus interested a group of first year BBA students of DBS and they decided to set up this company. Salads and fresh fruit juices and health drinks have been making a lot of rounds across various circles, but general public have not yet bought into the idea of having salads as main course meals. This was the idea behind setting up the Salad bar as a campus company that would allow the entrepreneurs to experiment the concept and then set this up as a full-fledged salad bar competing with the likes of Dominos, Subway, etc.

The students who set up this venture include Ms. Shivani Sapolia, Mr. Nishant Kumar and Mr. Duggivalasha Vikas.

Company Overview
BMSW is a campus company where we serve our customers with exotic salads which are not only nutritious but delicious too.

Needs or challenges Addressed:
Migrated students studying in our college wandered here and there for nutritious and tasty food. This search usually leads them to costly junk food junctions or the unhygienic street food. So we tried to rule out both the options and decided to have our own New Salad Bar in the college campus.

Product Description:
We are offering different variety of salads like sprout salad, corn salad, salads with kebabs, etc. along with handmade hot & cold drinks. All our salads are available in Traditional Indian flavours.

Our USP:
1. Cost effective.
2. Introducing Indian flavours.

Market Description and Target Customers:
There are no competitors for our salad bar around our locality. Our target customers are students and the faculty of our college.

Operational Plan:
- We will purchase vegetables twice in a week.
- We will be working five days a week during lunch time.
- We will take orders.

Pricing:
Average price of the salad would be about INR 30 and a drink would cost INR 15 per glass.

Business Model Canvas

Key Partners	Key Activities	Value Proposition	Customer Relationships	Customer Segments
• Vendors for purchasing groceries • Public for developing newer varieties of salads • Delhi Business School for use of its premises • Other institutions for expansion of the salad bar	• Purchase of fruits, vegetables, powders and syrups • Culinary activities • Presentation of salads and drinks • R&D for new varieties of salads	• Health Conscious	• Direct relationships with customers	• Youth • Health conscious adults
	Key Resources • Refrigerators and microwave ovens • Stoves and utensils for preparing salads • Chefs and servers for serving the salads		**Channels** • One to one Direct Marketing, through a website	

Cost Structure	Revenue Streams
• Salaries • Marketing / Relationship costs • Printing and Stationery, publishing materials • Purchase of refrigerators, utensils, ovens and stoves • Internet	• Revenues sale of salads and drinks

Marketing and promotional strategy:

- Print menu brochures to share with the students and faculty of the school.
- Create a website and use social media, specifically Facebook for inviting user comments on dishes that we prepare and solicit feedback on the services offered and ways to improve the offerings
- Sponsor events in the school fests
- Special discounts would be offered on combos.
- We propose to introduce one new dish every month.
- We shall also welcome new recipes from our customers. If their recipe gets selected, then the recipe would be named after the creator of the recipe.

Future growth strategy:

We will be starting our salad bars in nearby college campuses soon and we have a vision of starting a chain of BMSW all over India.

Competitive strategies:

The closest competitor of our business is Subway. While Subway focuses on sandwiches, our main focus will be on consumption of raw fruits and vegetables which are healthier. The competitive strategy shall include setting up a chain of salad bars across the country through franchising.

Back of the envelope calculations

Average Price Per plate	INR 30
Average Price per glass	INR 15

We hope to sell 3 plates of salad and 3 glasses of juices per day.

The contribution per day can then be calculated as below:

Plate	INR 90
Glass	INR 45
Daily Sales	INR 135
Weekly Sales	INR 945

Cost of raw materials, like fruits and vegetables, and other ingredients is expected to be about INR 420 per week

Total Variable Cost	INR 420

Fixed costs include cost of electricity, transportation among others. We expect this to be INR 1400.

Total Fixed Cost	INR 1400

Weekly Contribution	525
BE	2.666667 or 3 weeks

BE units	90

Key skills required:
- Good Presentation of Salads
- Impressive culinary skills
- Time management
- Knowledge of tastes of various ingredients used, specifically powders and syrups.

Socio-economic Impact:

We are promoting people to opt for nutritious diet.

Risk & Assumption:

Students have aversion from salads. So the greatest risk would be to change such mind sets.

Exit Strategy

The exit strategy would be to sell the business to an established chain, like Dominos, Café Coffee Day or Barista and the like.

The promoters of the company invested INR 10,000, in setting up the infrastructure in the DBS campus, up from the initial amount of INR 1,400.

The promoters expected to sell 3 plates and 3 glasses of drinks per day, but ended up selling 30 plates of salads and 20 glasses of health drinks per day.

Thus, they broke even within 2 weeks, and ended up making profit in the first month. The projected operational expenses, revenue sheet is given below.

Projected Statements

Month	No. of customers	Price / plate	price / glass	Salad Revenue	Juice Revenue	Investments	RM Costs	Tptn Costs	Misc	R&D	total revenue	total expenses	Diff
Jan-12	45	30	15	1350	675	500	1350	400	150	100	2025	2500	-475
Feb-12	50	30	15	1500	750	0	1350	400	150	100	2250	2000	250
Mar-12	60	30	15	1800	900	0	1350	400	150	100	2700	2000	700
Apr-12	60	30	30	1800	1800	8000	1350	400	150	100	3600	10000	-6400
May-12	65	30	30	1950	1950	0	1350	400	150	100	3900	2000	1900
Jun-12	70	30	30	2100	2100	0	1350	400	150	100	4200	2000	2200
Jul-12	75	30	30	2250	2250	0	1350	400	150	100	4500	2000	2500
Aug-12	80	30	30	2400	2400	0	1350	400	150	100	4800	2000	2800
Sep-12	85	30	15	2550	1275	4000	1350	400	150	100	3825	6000	-2175
Oct-12	90	30	15	2700	1350	0	1350	400	150	100	4050	2000	2050
Nov-12	95	30	15	2850	1425	0	1350	400	150	100	4275	2000	2275
Dec-12	100	30	15	3000	1500	0	1350	400	150	100	4500	2000	2500
													8125
Jan-13	107	35	20	3745	2140	0	1500	450	200	100	5885	2250	3635
Feb-13	115	35	20	4025	2300	0	1500	450	200	100	6325	2250	4075
Mar-13	122	35	20	4270	2440	0	1500	450	200	100	6710	2250	4460
Apr-13	131	35	20	4585	2620	0	1500	450	200	100	7205	2250	4955
May-13	140	35	20	4900	2800	0	1500	450	200	100	7700	2250	5450
Jun-13	150	35	20	5250	3000	0	1500	450	200	100	8250	2250	6000
Jul-13	161	35	20	5635	3220	0	1500	450	200	100	8855	2250	6605
Aug-13	172	35	20	6020	3440	0	1500	450	200	100	9460	2250	7210
Sep-13	184	35	20	6440	3680	0	1500	450	200	100	10120	2250	7870
Oct-13	197	35	20	6895	3940	0	1500	450	200	100	10835	2250	8585
Nov-13	210	35	20	7350	4200	0	1500	450	200	100	11550	2250	9300
Dec-13	225	35	20	7875	4500	0	1500	450	200	100	12375	2250	10125

78270

Month	No. of customers	Price / plate	price / glass	Salad Revenue	Juices Revenue	Investments	RM Costs	Tptn Costs	Misc	R&D	total revenue	total expenses	Diff
Jan-14	241	40	25	9640	6025	0	1650	500	250	100	15665	2500	13165
Feb-14	258	40	25	10320	6450	0	1650	500	250	100	16770	2500	14270
Mar-14	276	40	25	11040	6900	0	1650	500	250	100	17940	2500	15440
Apr-14	295	40	25	11800	7375	0	1650	500	250	100	19175	2500	16675
May-14	315	40	25	12600	7875	0	1650	500	250	100	20475	2500	17975
Jun-14	338	40	25	13520	8450	0	1650	500	250	100	21970	2500	19470
Jul-14	361	40	25	14440	9025	0	1650	500	250	100	23465	2500	20965
Aug-14	386	40	25	15440	9650	0	1650	500	250	100	25090	2500	22590
Sep-14	414	40	25	16560	10350	0	1650	500	250	100	26910	2500	24410
Oct-14	443	40	25	17720	11075	0	1650	500	250	100	28795	2500	26295
Nov-14	473	40	25	18920	11825	0	1650	500	250	100	30745	2500	28245
Dec-14	507	40	25	20280	12675	0	1650	500	250	100	32955	2500	30455

249955

Questions

1. Do you think the idea was feasible to be set up as a campus company?
2. Do you think the research on the idea was adequate? If you were to help the entrepreneurs on the research, what would you suggest to the entrepreneurs?
3. Do you think the pricing is adequate for the salads and health drinks?
4. Does the business model canvas capture the various elements of the venture?
5. Do you think the entrepreneurs have the necessary skills to execute the business?

Uthaan

Executive Summary

Uthaan is a not-for-profit organization that is being set up focusing on the following areas:

1. Educational benefits to children below poverty line
2. Health awareness and education among women

The above mentioned aspects are problems that are faced by the society at large and there are various schemes of the Government that focus on these areas.

Himachal Pradesh, being one of India's fastest growing small hill states. But, we find that there are a lot of problems faced by women and children, in addition to senior citizens. The literacy rate among women in HP is quite high, as compared to the national average. According to the 2011 census, the literacy rate of women in HP is 76.6%, against the national average of 65.46%. The literacy rate of women is important for the development of the society, allowing her to keep herself healthy and create an educated society. In spite of such a high literacy rate, a large percentage of women are still not aware about their health.

In addition to the issues faced by women, there are a number of migrant children who have no access to quality education. Some of the children of these migrant families go to the Government Schools in HP, but a number of other children of these migrant families do not have the privilege of going to a school. These children cannot afford school fees, purchase books and uniforms among others and their parents do not earn enough money to afford sending their children to schools.

The Government of HP is taking steps to encourage these children to attend schools, by providing them with uniforms, mid-day meals, free books and iron tablets, but still the situation has not improved. We intend to adopt these schools and focus on educating these children.

Our future growth will focus on some critical issues faced by society, like domestic violence against women, female foeticide, drug abuse, AIDS, disaster management and sustainable development, among others.

Market Opportunity and Size

A not-for-profit organization represents a key factor in the development of a strong civil society. The market size of not-profit-organizations is growing every day and has been occupying an important place in the market / society.

An opportunity for a social enterprise can be identified from various societal issues, like drug abuse, saving the girl child, women's health awareness, etc.

An opportunity can be grabbed out of these issues and a solution can be identified for the above issues by forming a social enterprise.

Since our focus is on children's education and women's health issues, let us identify the market opportunity for these areas in Himachal Pradesh.

In HP, the number of families below poverty line is quite low, as compared to other states.

HP has a total population of 6,856,509 (68.56 lakhs as per the 2011 census). The percentage of population below poverty line is 7.63% (approximately 5.23 lakhs). This is our market size, and our aim is to educate these students and make these families aware of their health and sanitation facilities.

Our offerings

The main purpose of setting up our social enterprise is to solve various societal issues, due to various reasons like poverty, lack of knowledge, illiteracy, etc. the main offerings will be delivered by our social enterprise include:

1. Catering to the educational needs of children below poverty line by providing educational benefits to them. The children of migrant labour who want to study but cannot afford due to their financial background. To achieve this, we will adopt schools and employ qualified teachers as volunteers to teach these children.
2. Provide health and sanitation awareness to women, with a specific focus on illiterate women.
3. Later, we shall foray to setting up of old age homes.

Competitive landscape

Our competitive landscape consists of the following five factors.

Threat of substitute products / services: there are a number of social organizations already offering these services.

1. Threat of new entrants: India being a very large country, there is immense opportunities for new entrants to offer such products and services

2. Intensity or Rivalry of Competition: being a social enterprise, competition is not a focus, but we would look at having collaborations with our competitors. Thus, we would like to eliminate competition by collaborating with other social enterprises.

3. Bargaining Power of Suppliers: Suppliers for a social enterprise includes stationery and other materials used for operating a school and providing material for health awareness for women. The bargaining power of suppliers would be low due to the fact that today many corporates are required to spend a percentage of their profit on corporate social responsibility. Thus, bargaining power of suppliers is low.

4. Bargaining power of Buyers: Bargaining power of buyers is low, because they do not buy anything and thus, this will not be applicable to them.

Business Model Canvas

Key Partners	Key Activities	Value Proposition	Customer Relationships	Customer Segments
• Government • Government Schools • Other NGOs	• Provide education to children of migrant labours • Adopt Government schools • Educate women about their health	• Education and Empowerment	• Direct relationships with customers and consumers	• Children • Women
	Key Resources • Field researchers • Computers, software and website • Teachers for adopted schools • Trainers for providing women awareness about their health		**Channels** • One to one Direct Marketing, through a website	

Cost Structure	Revenue Streams
• Salaries • Relationship costs • Printing and Stationery, publishing materials • Purchase of fixed assets and educational material	• Donations from corporate houses • Government funding for adopting schools

Marketing Plan

The marketing plan for this social enterprise shall include

1. Talking to government schools for adopting them
2. Discussing with the Government and identifying schools for adoption
3. Engaging in ground level research for identifying health issues faced by women
4. Engaging with organizations that offer women's healthcare products
5. Developing a portfolio of offerings
6. Engage corporate houses for receiving CSR funds

Financial Plan

The financial plan for the social enterprise is as given below:

Sources of revenue

Funding from corporate houses like SJVNL, Infosys and Millennium Alliance, among others. Government funding for adopting a school

Investments

Purchase of assets like furniture, computers, etc.

The table below gives the break-up of costs, investments and revenues for our social enterprise.

Items of expenditure	Amount (INR)
Purchase of fixed assets	600,000
Office furniture	50,000
Coffee vend	8,000
Filter	5,000
Website creation	10,000
Total	673,000

Revenue

Funding component	Amount (in INR)
Funding from corporate houses (annually)	1,000,000
Funding from government for adopting schools	1,500,000
Total	2,500,000

Risks and Mitigation

The three main disks faced by a social enterprise are

1. Shortage of funds
2. Lack of project management experience
3. Product manufacturing and selling experience

The most important risk faced by an NGO is shortage of funds. The funds generally issued by the government are not enough and adopting a school involves a lot of paperwork.

Secondly, when a new social enterprise is to be started, lack of project management knowledge hinders managing new projects and utilizing funds. In order to mitigate these risks, we will take the following steps.

1. Use women self-help groups to manufacture products through cottage industry schemes, that could be sold in the market and the revenue generated could be used for growing the organization. Products that could be produced include hosiery items, stuffed toys, home-made soaps and toiletries, pickles and candles, among others.
2. Get our team trained in various project management techniques and hire experts in project management to manage our projects.
3. In addition, we will also hire field researchers to research various issues faced by women and children so that we can provide solutions based on the output of these research reports.

Team

Our team consists of two MBA graduates.

1. Ankita Sharma. She holds a Bachelor's Degree in Business Administration and a Master's Degree in Business Administration from APG Shimla University. Her vision is to set up a social enterprise focusing on women and children, develop and implement strategies for their development, education, empowerment and health.

2. Rupali Thakur: She holds a Bachelor's Degree in Commerce and a Master's Degree in Business Administration from APG Shimla University. She is keen to take up a role in fund raising for social enterprises, and get involved in developing strategies for developing, educating, empowering women and children, leading to the development of the society in particular and the country in general.

Questions

1. Have the entrepreneurs identified the problem area effectively?
2. Do the entrepreneurs have clarity about their funding strategies?
3. How can you improve on the financial plan of the social venture?
4. Is the marketing plan and strategy adequate for the venture?
5. Does it make sense for the entrepreneurs to review the competitive landscape?

LiftLo

Executive Summary

Highlights

LiftLo bike renting service offers tourist an exquisite experience of having a personal bike, where there will be no boundaries for exploration, and now they don't have to rely on any tourism agencies and itinerary for making their holidays memorable. No cheats and frauds. Our customer service will always be there to guide them where ever they go.

Objective
LiftLo offers,
1. Cheap and efficient way of transportation facilities to the tourist.
2. Independent and hassle free driving.
3. Give a room to tourist for exploration and free-way riding.

Mission Statement
To be the first largest bike renting group, we would like to see our customer happy and curious by providing them excellent service and guidance.

Company location and team members
LiftLo will operate from rented shop located at Agra, Mathura and Ajmer city. The company needs 1000 square foot building for office and garage set-up. We, Ankit Gupta, Sunil Kumar, and Hrushikesh Singh, all are graduates from IIT Mandi, will be the founders of this company.

Service
LiftLo is the exclusive dealer shop which provides rented bikes to tourist for site seeing in Agra, Mathura and Ajmer. LiftLo bikes comes with GPS tracking system and all security accessories like maps, helmets, raincoats, first aid box and tool box. We shall provide them full assist during their visit, and a 10 am to10 pm customer care number will be provided for their assistance and convenience.

Financial Planning
Initially we need seed fund of around INR 7 lakhs to start our business. We would start with marginally higher at INR 7.5 lakhs, which would be contributed by all the three members equally from past savings. We are avoiding bank loan because of hectic bank interests. Later, if there is a need for any financial support, we will look for bank loans.

Description of Business

Company Overview
LiftLo will be a full service bike renting service will be located in popular tourist spots it will be the only authorized bike renting in the city. The shop, which serves the large national/international tourist, caters to many different segments including: commuter and road enthusiasts. In addition to bike sales, the store has a full line of accessories, like helmets, apparels, and tourist maps/guide. The shop will take part time rented mechanics to provide repairs and installations for customers.

Location

At initial phase, we will look for popular tourist attraction where tourist doesn't have any good transport options. In our initials findings, city like Agra, Mathura, and Ajmer will be on our first priority.

We will establish our main head office in Agra and two subsidiary offices in Mathura, and Ajmer. Location of our office will be on popular tourist spots. Each office will have one room and a space for bike parking (capacity: 10-5 bikes depending upon location and demand). All office area will be on monthly rent basis.

Services

LiftLo offers,

1. Cheap and efficient way of transportation facilities to the tourist.
2. Independent and hassle free driving.
3. Give a room to tourist for exploration and free-way riding.

Hours of Operation

Our services will be active on all weekends and weekdays except Wednesday.

Our operating time:

Weekends: 10:00am-10:00pm.
Weekdays: 12:00am-10:00pm.

Service Delivery

1. Tourist will be offered bikes depending upon availability and his model preference.
2. Tourist have to sign a 'bike hiring agreement', which contains all terms and conditions, and have to promise for safe return of the bikes, and details about fines if he unable to do so.
3. Security deposit of INR 10,000 and a copy of the passport (if international tourist)/valid identity card (local tourist).
4. All the bike accessories will be provided like helmet and map.
5. A 10-minute free test drive will be offered to the customer to ensure that bike is running smoothly and will not cause any future problems.
6. All fuel expenses will be paid by customer.
7. Returning of bike with Final payment after a promised period.

Management

At present, we are three team members in the business. As soon as the operation is firmly established, we will look at employing a full time clerk. We will also look to using people on contract basis as the level of work increases. This area will be reviewed at the end of the first year in business, and decisions on further employees/contractors made on the basis of actual financial results.

Revenue Sources

LiftLo has two primary ways of generating revenue: service and event organization. Tourist will pay rent in expense of bike renting service they are getting. Customers have to pay a base charge and he/she needs to return the bike at appropriate time, else they have to pay additional amount on excess duration of renting the bike.

Customer Benefits

LiftLo customers receive many benefits which are not present in traditional market. All new bikes come with GPS system and is provided with customer care number which ensure that customer can ask for guidance and route map wherever he/she goes. LiftLo follows 'UNBUNDLING' model where customers have their choices/interest where they want to go. LiftLo Bikes is also the only bike store in the area for road enthusiast as well as a full array of accessories. Additionally, LiftLo is very active in the biking community and offers tips and guidance to bikers. For competitive riders, the shop also offers discounts on service.

Business Goal

1. Setting up a trusted and liable brand image.
2. Establishing network within the city by connecting with various hotel/restaurant owners.
3. Understanding tourist needs and demand, and customizing business accordingly like buying bike popular bike model and go for premium bikes.

Business Model

Key Partners	Key Activities	Value Proposition	Customer Relationships	Customer Segments
• Restaurants and hotels • Travel agencies • Ad agencies	**Key Activities** • Bike Renting • Low cost transport service	• Experience	• Direct relationships with customers and consumers	• College Students • Honeymoon Couples • Foreign tourists
	Key Resources • Bikes • Mechanics • Fuel retailers		**Channels** • One to one Direct Marketing, through a website and hotline numbers • Channel partners like travel agencies, radio and TV channels	

Cost Structure	Revenue Streams
• Salaries • Purchasing and maintenance of bikes • Printing and Stationery, publishing materials • Purchase of fixed assets • Development of websites	• From renting bikes • From organizing biking and bike riding events

Market Analysis
LiftLo primary target market consists of students, couples, and bike enthusiast. This segment is made of 18-30 year olds that are active and love exploring and travelling. As the tourist areas are generally crowded and relatively confined, people would prefer bikes rather than existing auto and bus services.

Market Size

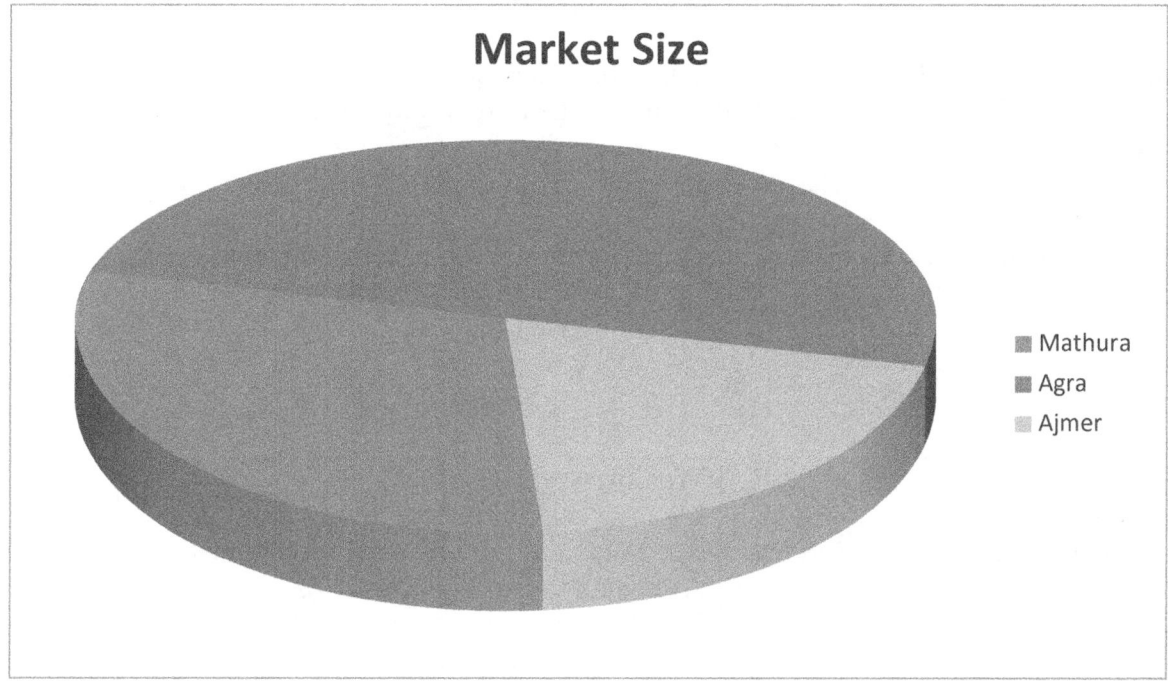

At peak season, mainly during holidays, Agra attracts around 5-8 lakh tourists, and 20-22 lakhs tourist every year. Similarly, with Ajmer and Mathura, every year around 10-12 lakh tourists visit this place, which prove to be a huge market for our operation. Since we are mainly targeting students, couples and bike lovers this limits our market size in around 20-30% of total tourist visit particular year, which comes around 4-5lakhs tourist in Agra, and 2-3 lakhs tourist in Mathura and Ajmer city, which is sufficient for our business to grow.

Market Trends
The bike renting market would have a potential to evolve. Lack of efficient transport facility and mal-practices by local tourism agencies, people are switching for some reliable sources regardless of thinking about it cost. The rise of branded tourism agencies like SOTC, makemytrip.com, shows a trend that people are more concerned about service and they want to make their every trip memorable. They look for privacy and personal space. This may cause an increase in demand for LiftLo bike services. Service sales may also increase as customers generally come for a short period, and they want to cover maximum tourist spots as possible. In such a scenario a bike can provide better alternatives to meet their expectations.

Competition

Direct competition in biking service is low. There are very few options for tourist at these locations. Currently few tourist bus services/rented taxi services are available, which are costly and don't provide customers with customized itinerary. LiftLo is expected to have a strong network with hotel/restaurant managers which will provide it with a competitive edge.

Indirect competition from local commutation services like auto-rickshaw/local bus service is expected to be high as it will provide a cheaper mode of transportation in case customers come in a group.

Competitive Advantages

LiftLo has several competitive advantages, including location, cost effective, customer care service and an established organization. Existing alternatives are not able to match these capabilities.

SWOT Analysis

Strengths:	Weaknesses:
Location near tourist place;	Less market during off season;
Cheap alternative to existing tourism services	Not suitable for family and group tourist;
Personal space for exploration;	Accidents and security issue;
Customer care network.	Weather problems;
	New in the marketplace.
Opportunities:	**Threats**:
Rising tourism market;	Legal issues;
Events and races will attract new customers.	Resistance from local commute services.

Marketing Strategy and Implementation

Internet Strategy

LiftLo does not intend to use its internet presence to drive retail sales, like so many other e-commerce sites. Rather, the company focuses on the immediate needs of its customers and the ability to fulfil those needs rapidly. A web site will include the store location and hours, promotions, local trails and links to related sites. Customers will also be able to research each bike and brand that LiftLo rent allowing customers to make better purchasing decisions.

Marketing Strategy

An aggressive marketing strategy will be employed that will leverage the location of LiftLo and the tourist who are most interested in biking. The company will have collaborations with few hotel and restaurant owner, company will promote them in terms that they will promote us in return. The company will also advertise in the local newspapers and promote events through the activities from taking permission from local government bodies.

Sales Strategy

Sales in the bike industry are bit cyclical varying with season and weather. Particularly sale will be low in monsoon and will be in full swing in summer vacations spring when students prefer to be outside and marriage seasons. Staffs will be motivated by sales bonuses of each bike rented.

Operational Strategy

Three of us will look over the sales in each city. We will oversee daily transactions as well as bulk marketing and day to day inventory changes. Initially, we do all the clerical and manager job by ourselves, when our business goes mature, then we look will adequately trained people in field of knowledge of sales and distribution as well as customer handling skills. They will also be technically trained in responding to the walk talky calls made by customers when they get stuck somewhere. We will have our working hours from 10am to 10pm and reduce working hours in monsoon season.

STRATEGIC ALLIANCES
1. Second hand bike providers
2. Honeymoon package providers
3. State universities student unions

Goal

Provide convenient, sporty services to young university studying students and all bike enthusiasts. Organize regular group rides to meet new people and build customer relationships

Financial Plan

Start-Up Expenses

I. Cost of Bikes	INR 4,00,000
II. License and Insurance	INR 40,000
III. Repair	INR 1,00,000
IV. Other expenses	INR 20,000
TOTAL STARTUP EXPENSES	INR 5,60,000

Determining Variable Cost

V. Rent	INR 1,20,000
VI. Electricity Bill	INR 5,000
VII. Telephone Bill	INR 3,000
VIII. Other expenses	INR 7,000
IX. Repairing of bikes	INR 25,000
TOTAL VARAIABLE EXPENSES	INR 1,60,000

Requirements

In order to launch LiftLo successfully with the required inventory and staff, the company will need INR 7,500,000 in capital. This amount is arranged with saving account of entrepreneurs. Bank loan is neglected here to avoid hectic interest rates.

Use of Funds

Funds are used to develop LiftLo. Initially funds are used to avail office and garage so we will purchase an adequate amount of inventory, including bikes, accessories and apparel. A portion of the funds will be used for a grand opening marketing campaign. This start-up needs around INR 600,000 of the initial capital. The remaining cash will be used for working capital for wages, rent, utilities and operational costs for the first year of business.

Income Statement Projections

Fare for one bike: INR500
Total working day: 26
Total bikes: 20

No of bookings (per day)	Total collection (in INR)	Variable cost (in INR)	Difference (in INR)
10	1,30,000	1,60,000	-30,000
11	1,43,000	1,60,000	-17000
12	1,56,000	1,60,000	-4,000
13	1,69,000	1,60,000	6,000
15	1,95,000	1,60,000	35,000
18	2,34,000	1,60,000	74,000
20	2,60,000	1,60,000	1,00,000

Break Even Analysis

We can see from the table that breakeven point for our business is 13 bikes per day. Working for six days a week, we would have a total of 26 working days in a month. We can arrange monthly wages by renting at least 13 bikes per day. Going below 13 would be fatalistic for us and it would become difficult for us to survive in the market.

Projected Cash-flow

We expect holidays to be the peak time for LiftLo services. We expect have 20 bookings during these days, and for the remaining days of the week, we expect to have a minimum of 10 rentals. This will ensure that the daily break-even point of 13.

Important Assumptions
1. Bikes are well maintained.
2. Our ties-ups and collaborators continue to cooperate with marketing initiatives and events.
3. All transactions are made in cash nothing in credit.
4. Fuel prices remain constant.
5. The bike renting industry continues to grow or remains steady.

Risk and Mitigation

Risk Scenarios
1. Market risk: Market risk is very less. Tourism sector hasn't much declined even in recession periods in India. It is among the fastest growing sector with ample opportunities.
2. Competition risk: The business can easily be duplicated, hence prone to huge competition. Further coming of branded tourism company may provide a huge competition in terms of their ease and quality service.
3. Technology risk: Coming up metro in the city or e-cars can affect this business significantly.
4. Financial risk: Accidents or bike theft would be a fatalistic to this business, may incur huge financial loss, depreciation cost or rising mechanic prices can also be a causes of concern.

Mitigating Factors
1. Bikes will be given to those people who will have proper identity card or passport, to reduce the cases of theft. All the bikes will be provided with proper insurance.
2. Keep a track of latest technologies, may look for investment in e-bikes sector.
3. Tracking system will be provided for real time location.
4. Expanding business by buying more bikes, look for VC's if the business performs well in first quarter. Induce values and improve quality of service, ultimately give this business a brand image.
5. Diversifying business, look for premium bikes services like Royal Enfield, and target local young college students. Promote it accordingly and Integrate riding bike with masculinity.

Our Team

1. Ankit Gupta
   B. Tech. Mechanical Engineering, IIT Mandi
   Look for business execution and legal affairs, manages office at Agra.

2. Sunil Kumar
   B. Tech. Computer Science and Engineering, IIT Mandi
   Financial planning, manages office at Ajmer.

3. Hrushikesh Singh
   B. Tech. Mechanical Engineering, IIT Mandi
   Customer relation and marketing strategies, manages office at Mathura.

Questions
1. How would you rate this business plan? Do you think it is a feasible plan to implement?
2. Have the entrepreneurs considered the financial aspects thoroughly?
3. How strong is the marketing plan? Is it adequate for this plan?
4. Do the entrepreneurs have the necessary expertise / experience to start this venture?
5. As a venture capitalist, would you invest in this venture? Why?

IndTours Pvt. Ltd.

Executive Summary

IndTours Pvt. Ltd. is a tourism service provider focusing on offering industrial tourism services and daily tour operations to students and general public alike.

With its head office in Shimla, HP, its vision is to bridge the industry-academia gap, allowing universities and industries to get linked through which students can understand the overall functioning of these industries.

The company intends to focus on all universities and colleges in Himachal Pradesh.

Market Size and Opportunities

There are a number of universities in Himachal Pradesh, but what the promoters of IndTours have found is that there are no opportunities for the students of these universities to visit many of these industries. It is found that there were 18 universities, including private universities and 96 colleges in the state.

In addition to providing industrial tourism services, the company also plans to operate daily tour operations from Shimla to Chandigarh.

Universities in Himachal Pradesh

The most important and critical market for the success of this company are the universities and colleges. While there are far too many colleges and it will not be possible for my team to indicate all of them. Hence, we are presenting a list of universities in HP for your understanding.

We are targeting the students of these universities for initiating our operations.

Name	Type	Location
APG Shimla University	Private University	Shimla
Arni University	Private University	Indora
Baddi University of Emerging Sciences and Technologies	Private University	Baddi
Bahra University	Private University	Waknaghat
Central University of HP	Central University	Shahpur
Chitkara University	Private University	Barotiwala
CSK HP Krishi Vishwavidyalaya	State University	Palampur
Dr. Y S Parmar University of Horticulture and Forestry	State University	Nauni
Eternal University	Private University	Baru Sahib
HP Technical University	State University	Hamirpur
HP University	State University	Shimla
IIT Mandi	Institute of National Importance	Kamand
Indus International University	Private University	Una
Institute of Hotel Management, Catering and Nutrition	State University	Kufri
Jaypee University of Information Technology	Private University	Waknaghat

Manav Bharti University	Private University	Kumarhatti
NIT, Hamirpur	Institute of National Importance	Hamirpur
Shoolini University of Biotechnology and Management Sciences	Private University	Solan
Sri Sai University	Private University	Palampur
University Institute of Information Technology	State University	Shimla

Offer

> ➤ Industrial tour services to students of universities and colleges, specifically engineering and management students.
> ➤ Daily tour operations for the general public from Shimla to Chandigarh and back.

Competitive Landscape

We have considered Michael Porter's 5-Forces Model to indicate the competitive landscape in which we will operate our organization.

Threat of new entrants: This is a business that requires no specific IPR like Patent or copyright. However, it can include a trademark, which we believe will come at a later stage, when our company gains traction and our logo gains appropriate attention to be distinguished as a trademark. Thus, barriers to entry are low or non-existent; in other words, the threat of new entrants is high. Since there are no barriers to entry, new players can emerge in this industry, and can compete with us.

Threat of substitute products: This service is not free from the threats of substitute products. Substitute products include travel by cars, trains or other means of public transport like taxis or government buses. The threat of substitute products is medium

Intensity or Rivalry of Competition: There are no real competitors at this point in time. However, as the business grows, we expect the intensity of competition to increase. Since the barriers to entry are also low, coupled with the intensity of competition, we expect that the competition will only rise in the years to come. While there are no companies offering this service specifically, we do see competition from existing tour operators, who operate outbound tours. With a little effort, they can even have tie ups with industries and operate industrial tourism services. Intensity of competition is medium to high

Bargaining Power of Suppliers: There are a number of suppliers, primarily suppliers from whom vehicles we intend to purchase. We expect the bargaining power of suppliers to be low to medium, because we have a choice, and we can look to negotiate on the price front.

Bargaining Power of Buyers: Offering excellent services would lead to buyers being ready to pay more for the better services that are offered. Thus, we expect the bargaining power of buyers to be low.

Business Model

Key Partners	Key Activities	Value Proposition	Customer Relationships	Customer Segments
• Universities • Colleges • Hotels • Industries • Petrol Pump owners	• Create link between industries and university & colleges through transport.	• Experience	• Direct relationships with customers and consumers	• College Students
	Key Resources • Drivers • Buses / Vehicles • Maintenance Crew		**Channels** • One to one Direct Marketing, through a website • Advertisements	

Cost Structure	Revenue Streams
• Salaries • Purchasing and maintenance of buses / vehicles • Printing and Stationery, publishing materials • Purchase of fixed assets • Development of websites	• Tour operations for students to visit industries • Bus operations

Risks and Mitigation

In this venture, we don't rule out the possibilities of accidents and other untoward incidents taking place. Given that we are planning to start these operations in Himachal Pradesh, the landscape here is subject to vagaries of nature, with cloud bursts and landslides being a very common phenomenon.

We expect the following risks to affect our venture. We have also included the ways to mitigate these risks.

1. Accidents: Accidents are the greatest risks that we expect to face on starting the venture. Accidents can take place when the bus/vehicle fails. In order to minimize accidents like these, we will ensure that the vehicles are well maintained, and safety measures are taken care of. In spite of this, there may be instances when things can go out of control. To take care of this, we would insure not only the bus, but all the students and other passengers who would be using our services. We would like to be the first tour operator providing insurance to our tourists and passengers, for a small premium.
2. Seasonal: We understand that our business will be seasonal in nature. Students would make an industrial tour only when they have their vacations, and to this extent, the operations become seasonal. In order to have continuous stream of revenue, we also intend to start regular bus operations between Shimla and Chandigarh, because we see a strong opportunity in this sector as many people travel between these two cities.

Our Team

Hans Raj – B. Com and MBA. Will handle the overall operations of the venture

Rakesh Kumar – BBA and MBA. Will handle the relations with Universities and Colleges

Maneesh Kumar – B. Com and MBA. Will handle finance and administration of the venture.

Questions
1. How would you rate this business plan? Do you think it is a feasible plan to implement?
2. Have the entrepreneurs considered the financial aspects thoroughly?
3. How strong is the marketing plan? Is it adequate for this plan?
4. Do the entrepreneurs have the necessary expertise / experience to start this venture?
5. As a venture capitalist, would you invest in this venture? Why?

Conclusion

I have presented only 4 of the business plans that my students have developed. While there were many other business plans that I wanted to develop into case studies, some of them backed off, due to the sensitive nature of their ventures, and that they did not want to share their information.

The remaining set of business plans would be presented in Vol. 2 of the book.

I would again like to take this opportunity to inform the readers that the contents of the case studies were developed by the students writing the business plans. I have only made a few changes to the business plans, so that the original thought is not compromised upon.

So, keep looking out for the second volume of this book on Case Studies in Entrepreneurship for all of you.

www.ingramcontent.com/pod-product-compliance
Lightning Source LLC
Chambersburg PA
CBHW080645190526
45169CB00009B/3504